AF575366

SOCCER LEGENDS

KURT WALDENDORF

childsworld.com

Published by The Child's World®
800-599-READ · childsworld.com

Photography Credits
Cover: ©Ben Radford/Getty Images; page 5: ©Matthew Lewis/FIFA/Getty Images; page 6: ©Matt West/BPI/Shutterstock; page 8: ©Bettmann/Getty Images; page 9: ©Pictorial Parade/Getty Images; page 10: ©Peter Robinson/EMPICS/Getty Images; page 11: ©Central Press/Getty Images; page 12: ©Phil O'Brien/EMPICS/Getty Images; page 13: ©Paul Bereswill/Getty Images; page 15: ©Andy Lyons/Getty Images; page 16: ©Vincent Laforet/Getty Images; page 19: ©Koji Aoki/AFLO/Getty Images; page 20: ©Christian Liebig/Corbis/Getty Images; page 21: ©Najmi Arif/Shutterstock; page 22: ©Nicolò Campo/Getty Images; page 23: ©Dan Mullan/Getty Images; page 25: ©Tom Hauck/Getty Images; page 26: ©Friedemann Vogel/Getty Images; page 27: ©Alex Grimm/Getty Images; page 28: ©AFP/Getty Images

ISBN Information
ISBN 9781503894273 (Reinforced Library Binding)
ISBN 9781503895232 (Portable Document Format)
ISBN 9781503896055 (Online Multi-user eBook)
ISBN 9781503896871 (Electronic Publication)

LCCN
2024941410

Printed in the United States of America

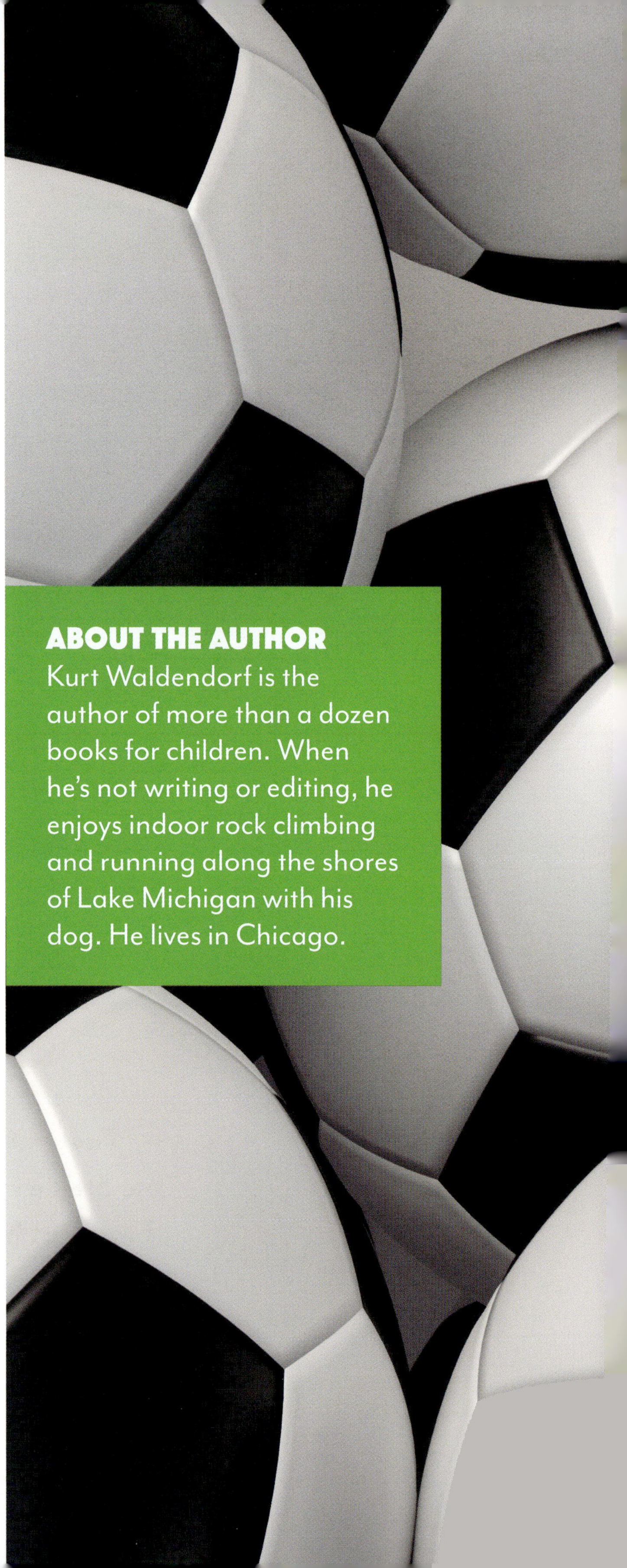

ABOUT THE AUTHOR

Kurt Waldendorf is the author of more than a dozen books for children. When he's not writing or editing, he enjoys indoor rock climbing and running along the shores of Lake Michigan with his dog. He lives in Chicago.

CONTENTS

CHAPTER ONE

WHAT MAKES A LEGEND?

Since modern soccer began more than 150 years ago, each generation has had star players. As the sport grew in popularity, some stars became known around the world. They became superstars. Among these players, a handful stood out above the rest. These players are remembered long after they are done playing. They are soccer legends. There are many ways a player can become a legend. But all legendary players have some things in common.

First, soccer legends are fun to watch. Some legends are known for their shooting or passing. Others stand out because of their speed or strength. Still others are remembered for their calm attitude or joyful excitement. No matter what makes the player stand out, each legend has their own style.

Christine Sinclair spent more than 20 years on Canada's national team. She is one of the best-known soccer players in the world.

Legends Cristiano Ronaldo (left) and Lionel Messi (right) have faced off almost 40 times. Combined, they have scored more than 200 goals for their countries.

Soccer legends also lead their teams to success. With a **national team**, a legend may bring their squad to a World Cup title or a gold medal at the Olympic Games. As part of a **club team**, they can make their mark by winning titles against the best competition. For men's soccer, the top leagues are in Europe and South America. In the women's game, the top leagues are in Europe and the United States.

Individual awards also add to a player's **legacy**. Each year, the Fédération Internationale de Football Association (**FIFA**) awards the top men's player and top women's player in the world with trophies. The top club players in Europe receive the Ballon d'Or prize. And at the World Cup, the best overall player wins the Golden Ball. The top scorer gets the Golden Boot.

However, players don't become legends just by winning awards. Players become legends by their actions on the field. This includes not only how they play but also how they treat others. By respecting their teammates, opponents, and fans, legends leave the game better than they found it. They inspire the next generations to do the same.

CHAPTER TWO

EARLY MEN'S LEGENDS

The first men's legend was Brazil's Edson Arantes do Nascimento, better known as Pelé. Pelé's career started early. At 16, he was picked for Brazil's national team. It didn't take long for him to make his mark. He scored a **hat trick** in the semifinals of the 1958 World Cup. In the **final**, he added two more goals to lead Brazil to victory. At 17, Pelé was the youngest player ever to win a World Cup. Over the next two decades, he became known for his amazing goals and joy for the game.

Pelé's family could not afford a soccer ball when he was a child, so he made one from a sock stuffed with rags.

Pelé scored 643 goals for Santos Football Club and led the team to 26 titles.

In all, Pelé won three World Cup titles. At the club level, he won six Brazilian championships and two South American championships. Late in his career, he helped make soccer more popular in the United States. He joined the New York Cosmos and led the team to a title. Pelé was later named Athlete of the Century by the International Olympic Committee.

As a player and coach, Johan Cruyff is considered one of the most important figures in modern soccer. His ideas influenced the way many teams still play today.

In the 1970s, a pair of legends changed the men's game. One was Johan Cruyff of the Netherlands. Cruyff was listed as a midfielder on his team's roster. But he often moved into different positions during the game to create scoring chances.

Cruyff's style of playing became known as Total Football. It allowed any player to be an attacker, midfielder, or defender. It also helped Cruyff win nine Dutch titles, one Spanish title, and three European club championships.

Franz Beckenbauer of Germany also used this style of play. He was listed as a defender. But he often attacked with crisp passes and long runs. Beckenbauer led his teams to four German titles and three European club championships. He is the only defender to win the Ballon d'Or twice.

Cruyff and Beckenbauer each had top moments at the 1974 World Cup. In the semifinals, Cruyff used dazzling footwork to fake out a defender. The move became known as the Cruyff Turn. It is still used today. But Beckenbauer took home the trophy. His defense in the final helped Germany beat the Netherlands 2–1.

LEGENDARY KEEPER

As the top scorers, midfielders and forwards often get the most attention from fans. But defenders and keepers are just as important to a team's success. Many believe Russia's Lev Yashin was the top keeper of all time. He changed how the position was played. Yashin roamed the penalty area, stopping the offense in its tracks. On the goal line, his quickness helped him make last-second saves. In 1963, he won the Ballon d'Or. He is the only keeper to win the award.

In the 1980s, Diego Maradona stepped into the spotlight. Early on, his success came with **club teams**. He won the Argentinian championship in 1981. In 1984, he joined SSC Napoli in Italy. At the time, the club was at the bottom of the league. In just three years, Maradona brought Napoli its first Italian title. Three years later, he did it again.

But Maradona's greatest moments came at the 1986 World Cup. Opponents could not stop the short, speedy striker. In the quarterfinals, he sprinted past four players. He then dodged the keeper and knocked the ball into the goal. The play became known as the "Goal of the Century." In all, Maradona scored or assisted 10 of Argentina's 14 goals at the tournament. Argentina won their second World Cup.

FROM PITCH TO PRESIDENT

On the field, George Weah became Liberia's first soccer legend. His great shooting and strong effort brought him to Europe's top leagues. He won the French and Italian championships. In 1995, he became the first and only African player to win the Ballon d'Or. But Weah's biggest successes came off the field. In 2018, he was elected president of Liberia. He led the country until 2024. Weah's son carried on his father's soccer legacy. Timothy Weah, who was born in New York, joined the US Men's National Team (USMNT) in 2018.

Diego Maradona played for Argentina in four World Cups. He led his country to victory in 1986.

CHAPTER THREE

THE FIRST WOMEN'S LEGENDS

Since soccer's early days, women have played an important role in growing the sport. But women's players have not had the same opportunities as men's players. For a long time, the women's game did not have a global tournament. That changed in 1991. The Women's World Cup began. Then in 1996, the Olympics added a women's soccer event. With these tournaments, women superstars had a chance to become legends.

American Michelle Akers was ready. In the 1991 World Cup, she tallied 10 goals. Two of them came in the final. She led the US Women's National Team (USWNT) to its first title. Akers was known for her long strides. She was an excellent striker. Later, she moved to midfield. She continued to shine. In 1996, she helped the US women win Olympic gold. And in 1999, she helped secure another World Cup win. When Akers retired in 2000, she'd scored 105 international goals.

Michelle Akers (in white) was named FIFA Women's Player of the Century in 2000. She spent 15 years with the USWNT.

Mia Hamm's 158 goals are the third-most of any international player—male or female. Hamm played in 276 games for the USWNT.

The United States had a second superstar in Mia Hamm. Hamm made her **debut** for the USWNT at age 15. She was good at scoring goals and could also set up scoring chances for her teammates with her passing skills. Led by Akers and Hamm, the USWNT dominated women's soccer in the 1990s. Hamm became one of the most popular athletes in the United States. In 2004, she capped her career with a second Olympic gold. She retired with four major championships and 158 international goals, a record for women and men at the time.

In the 1990s, the USWNT had a **rival** in the Chinese national team. China's team was led by Sun Wen. Sun was a speedy striker. She could score with either foot. Sun's top moment came in the 1999 Women's World Cup. In the final, she faced off against the dominant USWNT. Sun helped bring her team to a tie. The United States won the match in **penalty kicks**. But Sun earned the Golden Ball. Sun scored 106 international goals in her career. In 2000, FIFA named her the Female Player of the Century along with Akers.

CHAPTER FOUR

MEN'S LEGENDS OF THE 21ST CENTURY

On the men's side, new superstars were stepping up around the start of the century. One was Brazil's Ronaldo Nazário. At age 16, Nazário led his club to a Brazilian title. He then played in Europe, leading clubs to the Dutch and Spanish titles. Nazário was known for his dribbling and scoring skills. His joyful smile also made him a fan favorite. In 1996, he became the youngest person to win FIFA's Men's Player of the Year award at just 20 years old. However, his top moment came in the 2002 World Cup. He struck eight goals, earning him the Golden Boot and a World Cup title. In all, Nazário won two World Cups. He won FIFA's Player of the Year award three times.

While Nazário was becoming a legendary striker, France's Zinedine Zidane was becoming a legendary midfielder. Zidane was a tall, strong player. But he also had field vision and a great touch. This allowed him to create chances for his teammates.

Ronaldo Nazário was the youngest player ever to be named the FIFA World Player of the Year.

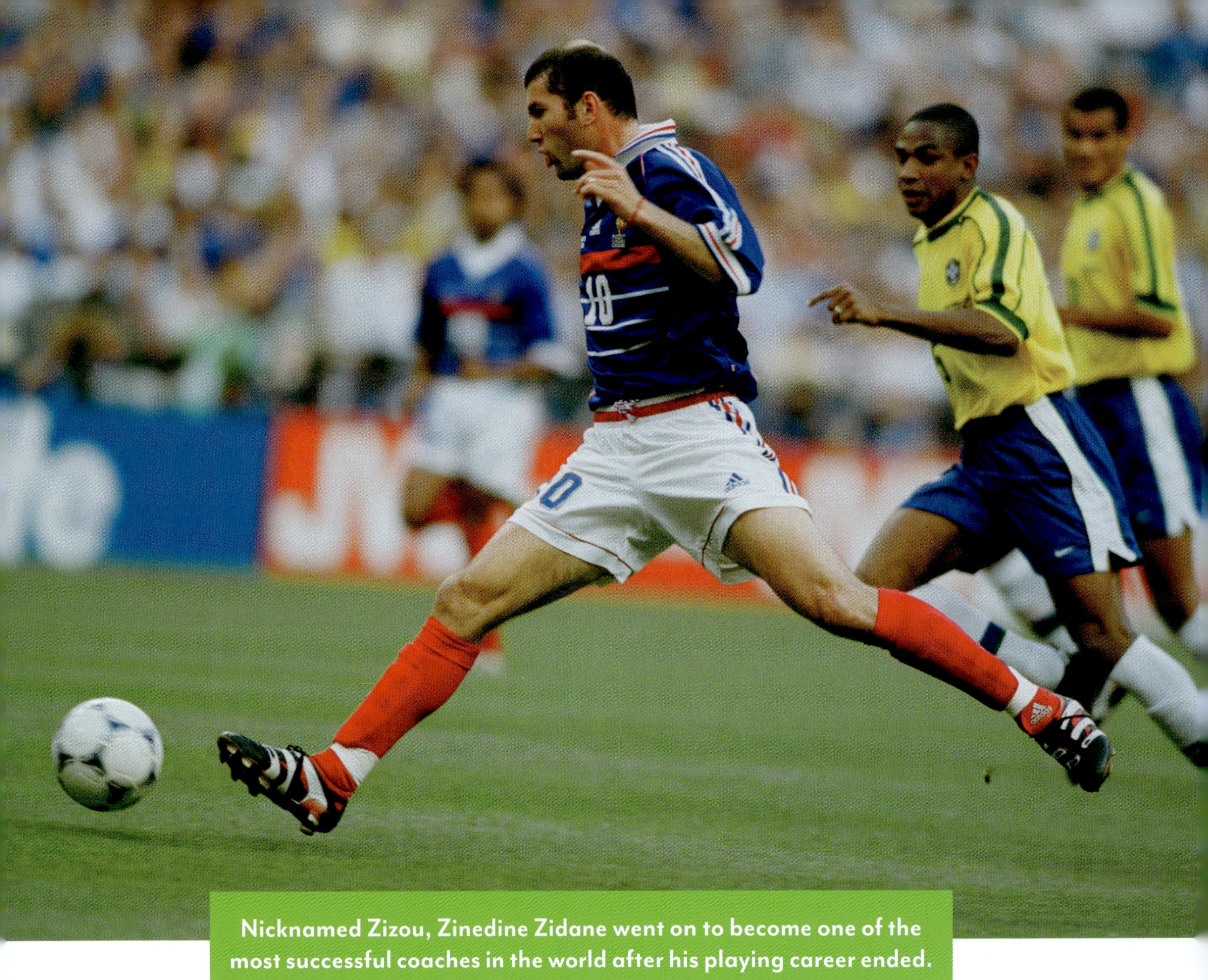

Nicknamed Zizou, Zinedine Zidane went on to become one of the most successful coaches in the world after his playing career ended.

Zidane's top moment came in the 1998 World Cup. In the final against Nazário and Brazil, Zidane **headed** two goals. His effort gave France its first World Cup title. Zidane also won at the club level. He earned a Spanish title, two Italian titles, and a European club title. Like Nazário, he was named FIFA Men's Player of the Year three times.

After Zidane and Nazário came another pair of legends, Cristiano Ronaldo of Portugal and Lionel Messi of Argentina. At age 18, Ronaldo joined top British club Manchester United. Ronaldo quickly became one of the best forwards in the game. He was an excellent shooter and could strike with either foot. In 2008, he led United to the European club title. Afterward, FIFA named him Men's Player of the Year. But that was just the start for Ronaldo.

RONALDO VS. MESSI

Ronaldo and Messi are the most decorated men's players ever. They have combined for more than 70 major titles. For nine years, the two played in the same league in Spain. In their head-to-head matches, both Ronaldo and Messi scored 23 goals each. Messi won more of the matches. He went 17–11 with six ties. However, Ronaldo has scored more goals in his career. He's first all-time, and Messi is second.

Ronaldo went on to win five European club titles. He added three English titles, two Italian titles, and two Spanish titles. In international play, he led Portugal to the European title in 2016. It was the country's first big international win.

Messi was Ronaldo's biggest rival. Messi was born in Argentina. At age 13, his family moved to Spain so he could train with FC Barcelona. At 17, Messi became the youngest player to score in Spain's top league. Messi was short and light. But he was strong. He moved with great control of the ball. In his second season, he led Barcelona to the European club title.

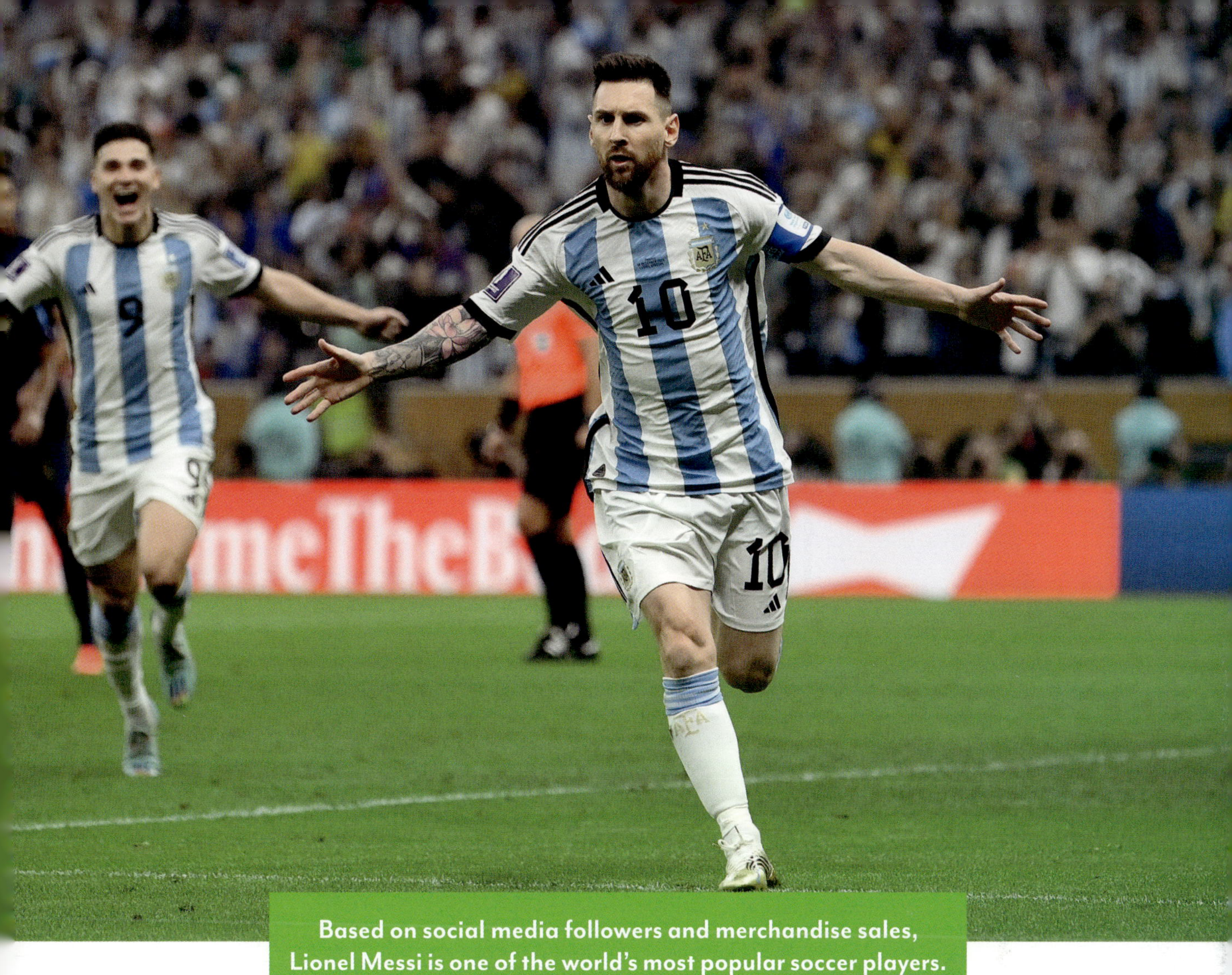

Based on social media followers and merchandise sales, Lionel Messi is one of the world's most popular soccer players.

From there, Messi continued to get better. He went on to win four European club championships. He added 10 Spanish titles and two French titles. But his top moment came in international play. In the 2022 World Cup final, he scored two goals in a thrilling win over France. For many, the World Cup win put him ahead of Ronaldo as the top men's player ever.

CHAPTER FIVE

A NEW ERA OF WOMEN'S LEGENDS

After the USWNT's dominance in the 1990s, a new era of women's players stepped up. One was Germany's Birgit Prinz. Prinz was a tall and physical striker. She had great fitness and a hunger to score. She showed these skills in her debut. At just 16 years old, she struck the game-winner in her first international match.

For the next decade, wherever Prinz went, titles followed. She led three different clubs to eight championship wins. She was named FIFA's Women's Player of the Year three times. But her biggest moments came at the Women's World Cup. In 2003, her squad upset the USWNT on the way to the title. In 2007, Prinz led Germany to its second straight Women's World Cup win. In all, she scored 14 World Cup goals and 128 total international goals.

Birgit Prinz won 22 titles with club teams, and 9 as part of Germany's national team. She scored nearly 400 goals for club and country.

Abby Wambach's 184 international goals rank second in the world—male or female. Only Christine Sinclair has scored more goals.

Abby Wambach joined the USWNT in 2001. She brought new life to the aging team. In the 2004 Olympics, she scored four goals. The last came in the final, winning the USWNT the gold medal. Wambach became known for her physical style. She was never afraid to go up for a header. Her most memorable header came in the 2011 Women's World Cup. She knocked the ball past the keeper with only seconds left in extra time, forcing a **shoot-out**. The USWNT did not win the tournament. But the play is one of the most memorable Women's World Cup goals of all time.

In 2015, Wambach capped her career with her first World Cup title. She retired with a whopping 184 international goals, breaking Mia Hamm's record.

While Wambach was bringing new life to the USWNT, Christine Sinclair was helping Canada become a top team for the first time. Sinclair was a dangerous scorer. But she also played midfield, setting up her teammates with accurate passes. Her biggest moments came in the Olympics. In 2012, Canada faced off against the USWNT. Sinclair shocked the world by scoring a hat trick. The US went on to win. But Canada's third-place finish was its best-ever result at the time.

JAPAN'S SOCCER LEGEND

In the 2011 Women's World Cup, the USWNT took on Japan in the final. Japan was led by Homare Sawa. Unlike some players, Sawa let her game do the talking. She was known for setting up her teammates with great passes. But she could also score. She totaled 83 goals in her international career. In the Olympic final, she scored in the 117th minute. Japan took home its first title. Sawa took home the Golden Ball and Golden Boot.

Marta, who began her career on boys' and men's teams, has been named FIFA World Player of the year a record six times.

In 2016, Sinclair again led Canada to a bronze medal. Finally in 2020, Canada won Olympic gold. In all, Sinclair scored 12 Olympic goals. When she retired in 2020, she'd scored 190 international goals, a new record for women and men.

The latest women's legend is Brazil's Marta Vieira da Silva, or "Marta." Marta made her mark playing on a club team in Sweden. In her first season, she led the team to a European club title. Marta became known for her amazing dribbling and superb scoring. She went on to win seven Swedish club titles and two US club titles.

Marta's top moment came in the 2007 Women's World Cup. She scored seven goals, earning her the Golden Ball and Golden Boot. Across six World Cups, Marta scored 17 goals, a record for women and men.

In 2024, FIFA created the Marta Award. The award goes to the best goal scored in women's soccer. Before the award was created, there was only a men's award for the best goal each year. The award is one small way Marta changed the game for the better. Just as the legends that came before her, she inspired the next generation to do the same.

GLOSSARY

club teams (KLUB TEEMZ) teams that represent an organization, often including players from many different cities or countries

debut (day-BYOO) a first public appearance

FIFA (FEE-fah) the international organization that oversees soccer competition

final (FY-nul) the last or championship game or match of a tournament that determines the event's winner

hat trick (HAT TRIK) the scoring of three goals in one match by one player

headed (HEH-did) used one's head to direct the ball

legacy (LEH-guh-see) the long-lasting impacts of individuals' careers or lives

national team (NASH-uh-nul TEEM) team that represents a country, in which all players are from a single nation

penalty area (PEN-uhl-tee AYR-ee-uh) a large area marked in front of the goal, where a foul by a defender results in a penalty kick

penalty kicks (PEN-uhl-tee KIKS) free kicks taken at the goal after teams commit fouls or to decide a match's winner after extra time

rival (RY-vuhl) a team that competes with another team for superiority

shoot-out (SHOOT-owt) a tie-breaker that involves each team taking penalty kicks

FAST FACTS

- Pelé scored more than 1,200 goals in his career. But many came in games that were not part of an official tournament, so they are not counted in his official total.
- Franz Beckenbauer is one of only three people to have won a World Cup both as a player and as a manager.
- In the 1986 World Cup, Diego Maradona played every minute of Argentina's matches, leading the team to the title.
- Abby Wambach scored more than one-third of her international goals on headers.
- Marta began her career playing on a boys' team because there were no girls' teams in her area.

ONE STRIDE FURTHER

- What sports legend do you find most inspiring? Write a paragraph describing the things that inspire you about them.
- What does it take to become a soccer legend? Create a list and have a friend do the same. Compare your lists.
- Ask friends and family members about their favorite sports. Keep track and make a graph to see which sport wins out.

FIND OUT MORE

IN THE LIBRARY

Davidson, B. Keith. *MLS*. New York, NY: Crabtree, 2022.

Everything You Need to Know about Soccer. New York, NY: DK Children, 2024.

Lowe, Alexander. *G.O.A.T. Soccer Midfielders*. Minneapolis, MN: Lerner, 2022.

Lowe, Alexander. *G.O.A.T. Soccer Strikers*. Minneapolis, MN: Lerner, 2022.

ON THE WEB

Visit our website for links about soccer legends:

childsworld.com/links

Note to Parents, Caregivers, Teachers, and Librarians: We routinely verify our web links to make sure they are safe and active sites. So encourage your readers to check them out!

INDEX